Touch The Poem

poems by ARNOLD ADOFF
pictures by LISA DESIMINI

THE BLUE SKY PRESS • AN IMPRINT OF SCHOLASTIC INC. • NEW YORK

For Bonnie

She Brings Me French Pastry So Light

Each Chocolate-Filled Delight Must Be

Anchored To The Bottom Of The Box.

I Have Just Time To Bite And Chew Before

They Float Away. I Take This Time

To Wipe My Mouth And Say A Smiling

Thank You: With Fingers, Teeth, And Poems.

A. A.

For Bonnie

L. D.

Touch The Poem

The Heel
Of The Palm
Of My Left Hand
Rubs Along The Bone Below My Cheek.
My Fingers Catch Along The Hair
Behind My Ear
As I Look At The O p e n Book
On My Table:
Each Poem
A Gentle
Touch.

Five

Ways   To Be Alone With An Itch

In The Center Of My Back

1.   Rub   Myself On The Corner Of The Hallway Wall.

2.   Roll   On the Family Room Carpet.

3.   Scratch   Myself With The Kitchen Broom Handle.

4.   Scratch   Myself With The Kitchen Broom.

5.   Drop   The   Cat   Down   My   Shirt.

Spring Saturday Morning

Legs Into Over Alls,
Feet Into S o c k s,
Toes F i n d i n g
T h e i r   Places:
I Pull   My Boots On
And Buckle   My Rain
Slicker All The Way.
I Am Ready With My
Black Rubber H a t.

I Do A Monster Walk
O u t s i d e
I n t o T h e M u d.

I
Close My Eyes

And Rub
The Palm
Of My Hand
On
Daddy's
Stubble
C h e e k.
I
Pull
His Rough
And Curling
B e a r d.
But
I Only Kiss His Fore
Head
Or His
Smooth
N o s e.

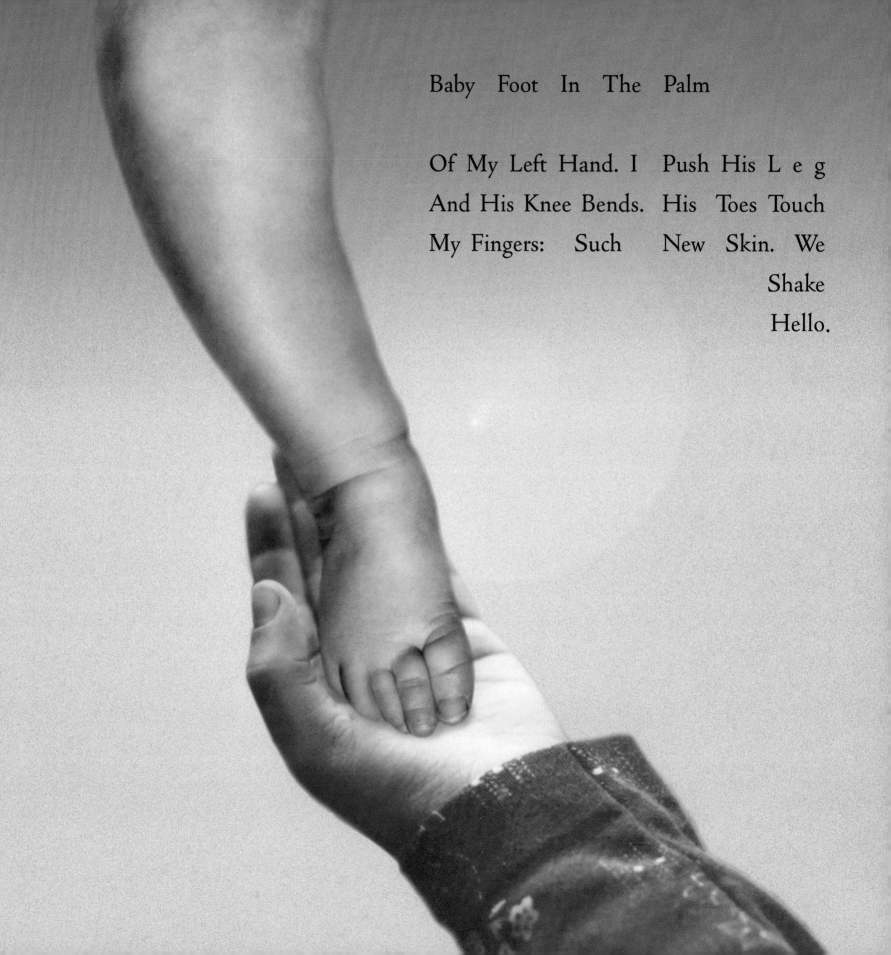

Baby Foot In The Palm

Of My Left Hand. I Push His L e g
And His Knee Bends. His Toes Touch
My Fingers: Such   New Skin. We

Shake

Hello.

Today   Is   The   Hottest   Day

So Far

This

Month.   But We Are   Watering

                                                  Watering

                                                  Watering

Tomato

Plants

Green

Beans

Green

Onion

Shoots.

The

Coolest   Water   Keeps   Running

Over My Hand And Down My Leg

                         And Down My Leg

                         And Down My Leg.

Ten Toes Grow   In Wet Ground.

Happy On The Beach

Here I Am
Happy On The Beach. My Feet Are Buried
In The Sand, Just Below The Burning Hot Top
Of The Sand: Where Toes Are Still Warm,
But Also Cool And Damp.

There Is An Ice Cube
In My Mouth, And When I Smile A Little,
A Drip Of Water Slides Down My Chin And Neck.

There Is JustEnough Breeze From The Bay.

My Fingers Dig.

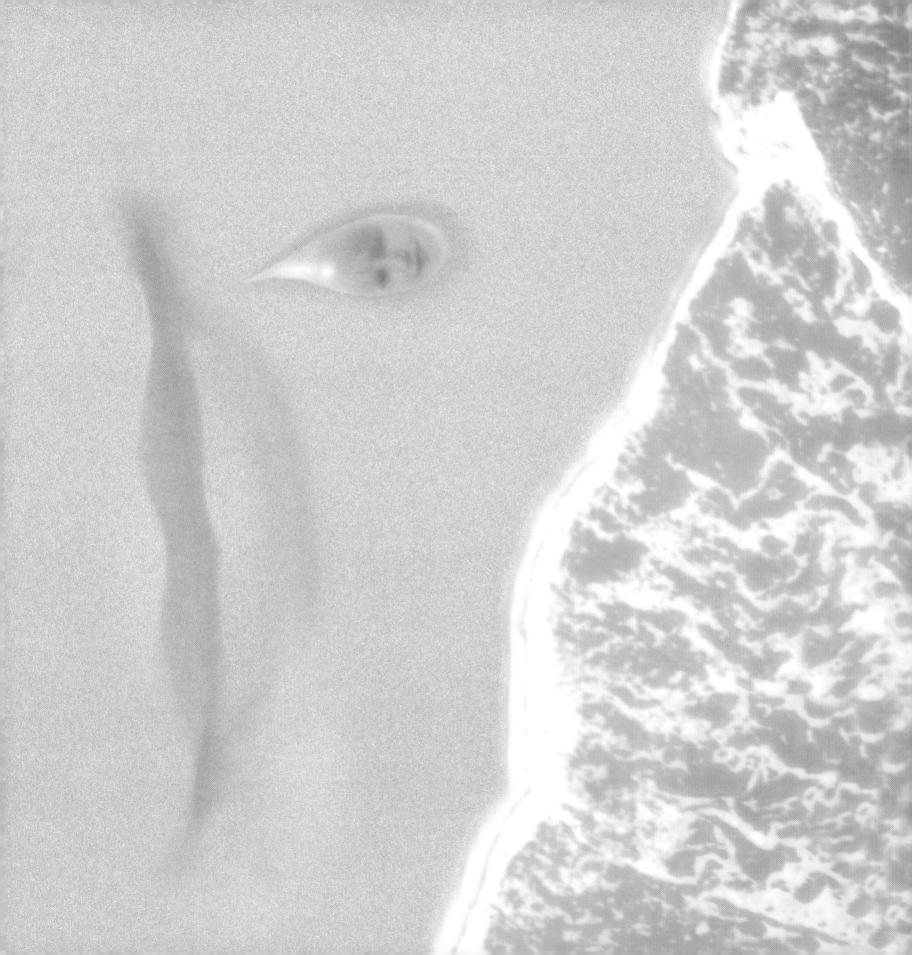

Fast Feel

Fuzz
Of Peach   Skin
                    Round
                        Rubs
My Upper Lip   Just
                Before
First
Bite.

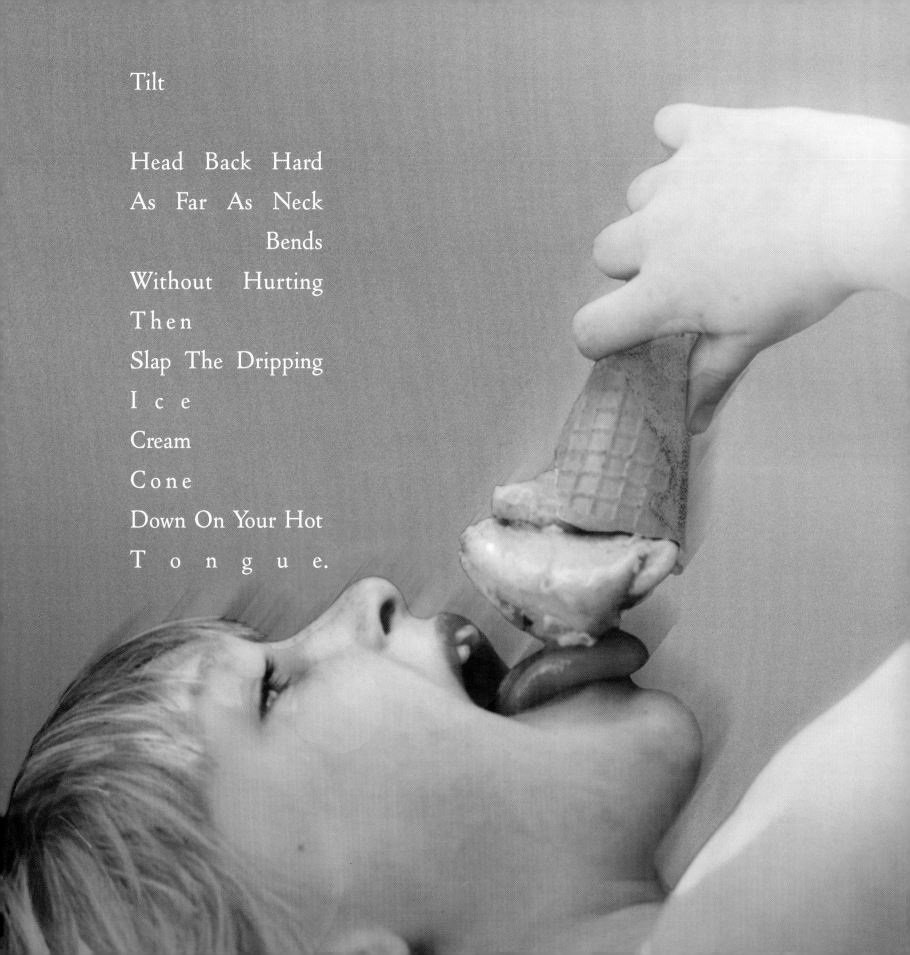

Tilt

Head Back Hard
As Far As Neck
          Bends
Without   Hurting
Then
Slap The Dripping
I c e
Cream
C o n e
Down On Your Hot
T o n g u e .

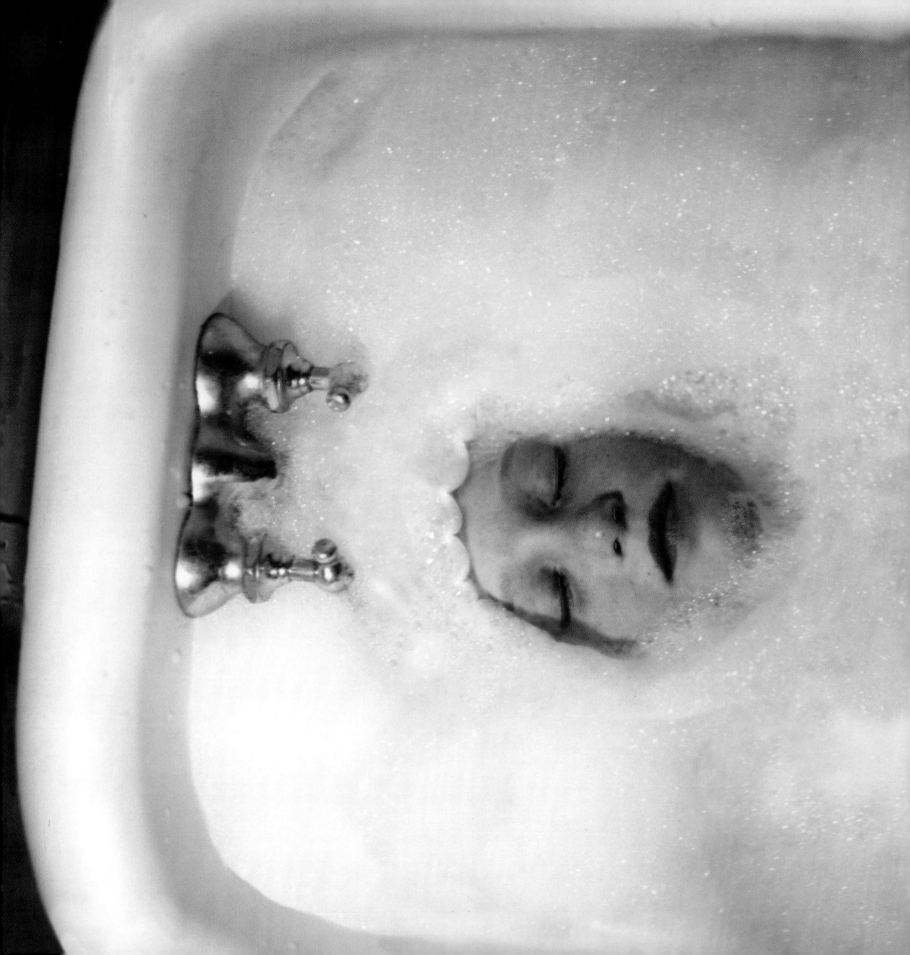

Tonight In The Tub

I Sit Up Straight
And Stretch Out My Arms
Until They Feel Their Floating:
Fingers Resting Very Still.

I Lean Back Slowly
Until My Long BlondeHair
Is All The Way Under The Water:
Water Surrounding My Forehead
Water Making A Liquid Crown
Water Covering Into My Ears.

Water The OneAndOnlyS o u n d.

Slow Slide

1. My Left Arm Reaches.
2. My Left Arm Reaches Out Too Far.
3. The Rest Of My Body Follows Fast.
4. There Is A Long Second In The Air.
5. The LeftSide Of MyHead Hits A Pile Of Straw.
6. The Rest Of My Body Follows Fast.
7. I Can Feel Each Piece Of Sharp Dried Grass.
8. My Left Arm Reaches.
9. My Left Arm Reaches Out To Wipe
                                    My Face.
10. My Right Arm Waves.

I Have New Garden Gloves

Soft   Leather   In   Back,
Palms   Of   Tiny   Black
Spots   That   Hold   Bats
And   Bike   Handles   And
Even   My   Momma's   Rake,
Her   New   Clay   Pots.

I Need This Solid Grip   As I Rock My Way
Into The Hall Of Fame   Playing   An Air
                                      G u i t a r,

Rolling
On My Back
In Leaves.

When We Do OurA r t

And   Finger   Paint:
                    We Paint
Our   Fingers   A n d
                    We Paint
Our   F   a   c   e   s.

The Girl Next To Me At Our Round Table
Has An Eye Patch C o v e r i n g Her Left Eye
And I Paint Very Carefully A Line Of Lashes
Curling Out Of Her Black Cotton Lid.

She Paints A Pirate Moustache On My Upper Lip.

I Always Know This Late Afternoon Time

After The Meal
Is Finally Over, And The Last Cranberry
Has Joined The Last Piece Of Turkey
From My Plate   To My Fork   To My Mouth.

I Always End Up On The Floor: My   Belly
Too Full To Stay In Front Of The Game,
My   Belly
Too   Full   To   Turn   Onto   My   Back.

Only The Smell Of Sweet Potato Pie Can
Lift
My
Head.

On

This

Coldest January Day In Bright Sun

We Play,

Knees On Ice

Until They Are Numb.

Your Hair Blows In The Wind.

My Wool Hat Itches, And The Sweat

Drips Down Behind My Ears, And Into Eyes.

I Wipe Wet Wool In W i n t e r Sun.

Sleep On Your Hand

And Your Whole Arm

Falls Asleep Under Your Heavy Head.

You Have To   Shake Out   The Pins And Needles

To Wake Yourself   All Up   All Over.

You Have To   Shake Out   The Pins And Needles

Through The Tips   Of   Your Fingers:

So You Can Wake Up Your Hand

In Time To Hold The Tube Of

T o o t h p a s t e   And Squeeze

Before You Drop The Brush.

My Forehead On Cold Glass Of Window

My   Nose   On Cold Glass Of Window.
My   Lips   Kiss   Perfect   Mouth   On

This

Frost

Face

Of Window.
We   Shine   Together   In   Dark   Night.

THE BLUE SKY PRESS

Special thanks from Lisa

to FIONA,

Tim, Zoe, Hannah, Asia, Heather, Esther, Sarah, and Cordelia.

The Blue Sky Press is a registered trademark of Scholastic Inc.

Library of Congress catalog card number: 95-34473

ISBN 0-590-47970-9

10 9 8 7 6 5 4 3 2 1   0/0 01 02 03 04

Printed in Singapore   46

First printing, April 2000

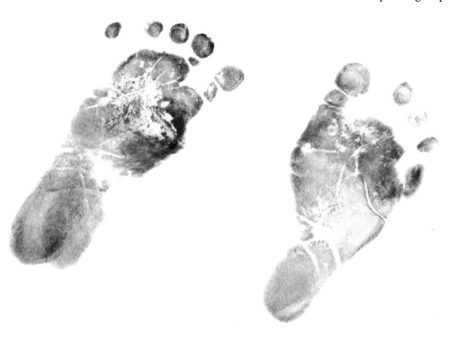